Prayers
Before an Awesome God

Prayers
Before an Awesome God

The Psalms for Teenagers

by David Haas

Saint Mary's Press
Christian Brothers Publications
Winona, Minnesota

To Art Zannoni, for continually opening me up to the richness of the Scriptures, and for his love, kindness, and support

To Jim Bessert, for the witness of his ministry, and for his support and friendship

To Kathy Leos; Ray East; Don Kimball; Anna Scally; Sr. Edith Prendergast; Leisa Anslinger; Jean Bross; Derek Campbell; Carol Dolan; JoAnne Cahoon; Jim McCormick; Sr. Dorothy Ederer, OP; Melanie Teska; Leon Roberts; Theresa Torres, OSB; Roberta Kolasa; Stephen Petrunak; Carol Porter; Tom Franzak; Bill and Dee Rustic; Jackie Witter; Joe Camacho; Thom Morris; Rob Glover; and Kathleen Storms, SSND; for what I have learned from them as they helped to awaken me to the cries of youth, and for being such wonderful partners in ministry

To Lori True, for her love, friendship, and tireless loyalty, and for constantly believing in me and my gifts

To Carl Koch, for being such a fantastic editor and for having the ability to help me sound coherent, and to all the folks at Saint Mary's Press

To my parents, and to my wife, Helen, for loving me through it all

Genuine recycled paper with 10% post-consumer waste. Printed with soy-based ink.

The publishing team for this book included Carl Koch, development editor; Laurie A. Berg, copy editor; James H. Gurley, production editor; Hollace Storkel, typesetter; Maurine R. Twait, art director; Cindi Ramm, cover designer; pre-press, printing, and binding by the graphics division of Saint Mary's Press.

Printed in the United States of America

Printing: 9 8 7 6 5 4

Year: 2006 05 04 03

Library of Congress Catalog Card Number

ISBN 0-88489-600-5

To Kate and Melissa Cuddy
   mother and daughter in faith
   partners in music and ministry
   keepers of the Word
   models and witnesses of kindness and generosity
   honored friends

Preface

Dear Friends—

The psalm-prayers
that you find in this book
are a gift from God.
They are for you.

It is amazing to realize
that God knows everything
that we are going through.
Even more exciting and awesome
is the realization
that God gives us prayers,
"tools"
to help us express and understand
what is happening within us,
and all around us.
These tools
can help us to really experience
completely
our humanity,
our vulnerability,
our fragile existence.

These ancient prayers are proof to us
that God has always been present
and attentive to us,
no matter the situation,
no matter the circumstances.

One of the wonderful things
about the Psalms
is that they represent every possible
human situation we can find ourselves to be in:
in these prayers
you will find ways to express
joy, excitement, hope,
contentment, peace, and confidence.

And in addition to that,
many of the Psalms give us a way
to voice our loneliness,
sadness, pain, anger,
even rage.

Yes, it is okay with God
to feel whatever we are feeling.
God wants to hear from us,
God wants us to vent and exclaim
everything that happens to us,
everything that we are going through.
Everything and anything—
you will find a path in these prayers.

These prayers are thousands of years old,
but remember,
no matter in what period of history
we find ourselves,
the same things are all around us:
happiness, joy, and pain,
guilt and healing,
forgiveness and acceptance.

Some of these Psalms
we pray and sing at church on Sunday.
Some of them will probably sound familiar.
Some of the Psalms, however,
we never get to hear
unless we take time to discover them.
It is also important to know
that originally,
the Psalms were always sung.
That is why they are so expressive
and filled with emotion.
But you don't have to sing them;
you can pray or meditate with them
in any way that is comfortable to you.

Reading from your Bible, the Psalms
can sometimes be difficult to understand.
Often there are references to places,
situations, and other events
that were unique to that ancient time
in which they were originally composed.

Some of the images still work well today,
some are difficult to relate to
in our present day and culture.
In this version
I have tried to find some new ways
to say the same things that another "David"
(and other authors from that time in history)
originally tried to express.

The Psalms have been a wonderful
touchstone for people throughout the ages.
They have certainly helped me in my life.
I am sure they can help you, too.

Remember that God is always listening.

David Haas

Psalm 1

To be happy,
stay away from those
who try to trick you.
Walk away from those
who make wrong choices.
Don't hang out with those
who are constantly negative.
But stay close to God,
learn about God's ways.

If you do, you will be
like a strong tree near the water,
blooming in full color,
with fresh leaves, and
with strong branches.

For those who walk away from God
will be blown around by every wind.
They will not be able to escape
the consequences of their decisions,
or be able to celebrate God's glory
as you do.
God will keep watch over us,
if we are strong and true.

Psalm 2

Why is there wrangling among you?
Why do you plot and scheme?
Throughout all time
those in power
have tried to oppose God
and those who follow God's way.

God laughs at such arrogance
and shows divine displeasure.

I continually share with you
God's law.
In fact, God told me:
"You are my children;
I give you new life.
All I have is yours."

Listen,
all of you who have power,
change your thoughts,
serve God,
be thankful,
be humble before God,
and remember who you are.
If you anger God,
you will not survive.
It is better for you
to find your safety in God.

Psalm

God,
so many around me
seek to hurt and harm me.
They want me to fail.
They tease and taunt me,
"Your God will not help you now!"

But that is not true.
You will be with me,
by my side.
When I call out to you,
you always answer.

So, I am able to relax at night,
sleep well, and know
that I will awake tomorrow
with you there to protect me.
When I think about this,
I am not afraid.

Stay close to me God!
Keep back those who would harm me.
May they suffer the destruction
of the evil they do.
Remember those of us
who try to be faithful to you—
and win over those who
struggle against you.

Psalm 4

God who created me,
when I am in trouble,
listen to me.
You always answer me
when I have problems.
You are always good,
and you consider my prayers.

Those of you around me
who follow the wrong way,
pay attention!
God always surprises us,
knows what's going on,
and never turns a deaf ear.

Remember that God is great,
but don't be afraid.
Listen to God's voice in your heart,
be calm at night,
and pray to God,
trusting always.

Those who don't believe will say:
"Who will give us the
good things that we need?
Even God has betrayed us!"
I do not listen to these voices,
for I know that you, God,
always bring peace.
I sleep well at night
for I know that you are with me.

Psalm 5

God,
I feel awful,
and I need you to listen
and to help me.

Every morning I will call on you,
and I will pay attention
to what you say to me.
Throughout the day
I will wait,
hoping that you will hear me.

I know that you hate evil, God,
so please,
keep it far away from me.
I know you reject the snobs,
liars, cheats, and bullies.
You despise those who choose violence.

But you are full of mercy
and forgiveness,
and because of this,
you let me be near you.
I can hardly believe it!

Keep me on the right road,
far away from those who wish to hurt me.
For you know they are guilty;
you catch them in the act
when they disobey your laws.

But when we trust you,
you give us reason to celebrate,
to have a party,
and to feel your protection—
safe always—
and so we praise you, God.

For you are always near
to those who follow your way,
and you shower us with good things.

Psalm   God, I know you are angry,
but please be gentle with me.
Go a bit easy on me,
for I feel exhausted.
Please take care of me,
for I am hurting inside.
How long will you
put me through this?

God of life, please save me
from all this—
you promised you would.

Every night I feel so
tired and awful.
I cannot seem to stop from crying,
because I'm afraid.

To all of you who want to harm me,
get away!
For God comes to me
and dries my tears,
and listens to me.

Psalm 7

God,
I feel safe when I am with you.
I need you to protect me
when I feel as though
I am being attacked.

If I have sinned,
then God,
I guess I deserve the pain
that comes from evil.

If not,
then pay attention
and crush those
who want to destroy me.
If you are just,
then come through
for me, God.
Give them what they deserve.
May my enemies be the victims
of the same evil they would do to me.

Help us to steadily live right.
You are just and fair to us.
When I am honest,
God will always defend me.
God will judge those who sin,
and they will face the music.

See how they scheme,
lie,
cause trouble.

Of course,
they make their bed and lie in it,
for it comes back to haunt them later.

Thank you, God, for your justice.
May I be thankful to you for that
forever.

Psalm **G**reat is your name, our God!
Everybody, everywhere
talks about how great you are!
You are wonderful,
and the news travels
across the globe!

Even children
laugh and babble about you.
Early in life
we find out how fantastic you are.

I see the result of your goodness everywhere:
the stars and moon at night,
the sun greening the earth,
the eagles and whales,
sparrows and dogs,
and all the creatures we rely on.
You create and arrange it all!

Why are you so good to us?
What have we done to deserve
such great things from you?
You have made us in your divine image.
You identify with us,
and we are fortunate
to receive the same glory
that we give to you.
You give us privileges and power
over all creation.
You are great, God!

May everyone know how awesome you are!

Psalm

Thank you, God.
I will never stop talking about you!
You are the reason I am joyful,
and you give me the voice
to sing of your goodness!
All those who are against me
cannot survive against you.

You keep me going,
and lead my enemies far away.
You have helped me
forget their ability to hurt me.

Destroyers, liars, frauds, and crooks
may win for a while, but,
finally, you wreck their plans,
frustrate their schemes,
and catch them in their own destruction.
With your help, my God,
I forget that they ever were here.

You never stop being God to me.
You are a constant reminder to me
that while others break promises,
you are always fair to me.

You take care of those
who are hurting and in pain;
you help them to be strong.
You never abandon us
if we keep trusting you.

Everyone should sing!
Everyone needs to hear
how great this God is!
God never forgets
those who are poor.

God,
when others come to jerk me around,
when I feel that I can't take it anymore,
you come and save me,
and because of that,
I will always be thankful to you.

You are so powerful
that even the most clever
cannot outdo you.

Bring us down to size
when we become too arrogant.
Help us to remember
that we are human.
That is enough.

Psalm

Where are you, God?
You seem to disappear
when I really need you.

Those who choose sin
seem to never feel sorry.
They cheat the poor
and rob the weak.
Others puff out their chest
and mock you, God.

They want us to believe
that there is no God,
that you are a figment of our imagination,
and that if you do exist,
you really don't care.
They do not want to believe
in a God that would keep them
from their selfish plans.
They think they don't need you,
so they lie, swear, and hurt others,
and everywhere they go,
trouble sets in.

They wait for an opportunity
to trick the innocent,
to steal from the elderly.
They think they can hide from you.

God,
don't let them get away with it
or give them a chance.
Show them that you exist,
bring them down.

We know that you
are constantly watching out for us,
and when the time is right,
you come to us
and help us through our struggles.

We trust you,
we trust you to be stronger
than those who are evil.
God, you listen to what we say
and give us reason to hope.
Then we will have reason
to be happy, and we know
that you will make things right.

Psalm

Listen everyone,
God is the one whom I will follow.
If you know this,
how can you expect me
to allow others to knock me down
and rob me of my hope?

God stays in place,
with all of heaven keeping watch.
God looks over us all,
deciding who is good
and who is sinful.
What God wants for us
is justice,
for God is just.

If we follow the way of God,
we will see God.

Psalm

God, help!
Stay, don't leave.
Everyone else has.
They did not keep their promises;
I feel betrayed.
The world seems filled
with gossips and liars,
people with twisted hearts.

You will get rid of hard words,
and you promise to bury
all broken promises with your goodness.

Then I will know you are speaking to me,
and you will hear the words
that I need to hear:
"When you need me,
I will be there."

Your word is good as gold,
the best.
Keep your word;
don't go back on what you
have said.
Keep us safe
and free from fear.

Psalm

Remember me, God?
If so, where are you?
How long
do I have to go through this?
Are you testing me?

God, enough is enough.
I want some answers—now.
I don't want to lose faith in you.
I don't want them to say,
"I told you so!"

I trust you, God,
and I will rejoice because you
always take care of me.

You are kind to me;
help me to keep singing.

Psalm

Ignorant people
say that you don't exist.
They use this as an excuse
to live in a way that is sinful.

You look upon us
to see if we are wise,
you wait for us
to reach out to you.

But it seems that no one
is trying to be good.
Everyone seems to treat people badly,
and they never pray.

If they were smart,
if they knew the depth of your power,
they would be shaking in their boots.
While we make fun of those less fortunate,
you make them feel wonderful and loved.

We need you to come and save us
so we can sing and be happy again.

Psalm

God, who are the ones that you welcome,
who are the ones that you call your own?

The ones who are close to you are
those who live lives that are admirable,
those who make the right choices,
those who speak the truth,
those who are courageous.
They speak the truth about others,
never spread lies;
they treat everyone well,
as each deserves.

They stay away from those
who demean you,
they rejoice with all who try
to stay close to you.
They keep their word,
they can be counted on.

When they give,
they give with no strings attached,
freely; they are generous,
totally for the good of all.
If we live like them,
we will never be shaken.

Psalm Keep me safe.
Only you can help me.
When I am honest,
I realize that you are what I need,
you are God.

I used to put my faith in things
and in people who always let me down.
I realize that now,
so I no longer
look to them for help.
I look to you, my God.

I bless you, God,
for you are my favorite teacher.
You teach me and lead me
every day, all day,
and if I am sure of anything,
I am sure that you are here with me now.
No one can convince me otherwise.

So how can I not be ecstatically happy?
I am happy with how you
keep me safe and filled with peace.
You will never leave me,
you will stay close to me forever
and keep me headed
in the right direction.

With that help
I know I will always be smiling!

Psalm 17

Hear me,
please hear me.
I really deserve some answers.
I have been faithful by praying to you,
and so I need you now
to help me set things right.

You have kept me awake at night
and tested me,
and I have remained faithful.
I have not lied,
I try to live the way you want me to.

Pay attention to me,
listen to what I am saying.

Show me the love that I have known before,
and keep watch over me.
Love me,
and keep me far away from those
who want me to fail.
They are cruel to me,
they speak badly about me,
they follow me,
waiting for the right moment
to watch me screw things up.

God,
I need you to take them on
and defend me from their bad intentions.
Use your power now,
I really need it.

Nurture me, God;
give me the power I need.
Then I will feel close to you
and be able to keep singing your praises
and know that you are with me.

Psalm

God, you are so strong!
God, you are love!
I lean on you all the time,
and you defend me from
the things that bring me down.
With you, no one can harm me.
Thank you, God!

I have often felt
that I could not make it,
that I would die.
During those times
I have cried out to you,
and you listened well.

You shake things up big time,
you can make amazing things happen!
In the midst of the most terrible storms,
you bring me through safely.
You keep me confident
when everything around me
gnaws at my self-esteem.
You help me breathe
when I feel my chest cave in from anxiety.
You fill my lungs with your loving presence.

I have always tried
to obey your commands,
to never drift away from you—
and you have rewarded me,
time and time again.

If we are good to you,
you are good to us,
and if we are honest with ourselves,
you deal with us the same way.
You rescue those who are sinking,
and lift up those who have been kept down.
You help me to see
when everything seems dark.
No one else can be God,
only you.

With you beside me,
I can accomplish anything.

You give me the energy I need,
and you prepare me for anything
that I might encounter.

No one is more supportive than you;
you give me everything I need
no matter what the situation.
You save me from those
who would violate me,
and you give me power over the ones
who would try to destroy me.

You are alive and well, God!
You are so good,
you always do the right thing!
I praise you more than anyone
or anything!
You always come through for me!
Blessed are you, our God.

Psalm   Everywhere I look,
I see your glory!
The news travels far and wide,
from morning till night.
Without anyone saying anything,
the word gets out about you!

You position yourself
for everyone to see;
the fire of your presence
is felt by all.

Your rules are perfect,
keeping us happy,
filling our heart.
You make everything clear,
and you always speak the truth.

Your word can always be counted on,
the thing we treasure the most.
When we keep your commands,
we experience blessings
too many to mention or fathom!

Keep us humble,
save us from our worst self,
help us face our fears,
keep us in your thoughts
and in your heart.
You are the rock we cling to—
keep us strong!

Psalm May God keep you safe
when you feel you are at war!
May God keep you strong!

May God bring forth the best in you
and be happy with you,
remembering what you need,
remembering what you hope for.

Then we will all be happy,
and we will celebrate,
thanking God for giving us
what we are dreaming of.

I know beyond all doubt
that God wants us to succeed,
and will reach out a hand
to help us through everything.

While some people boast of material things,
we brag about our God,
who is the best gift we could ever hope for!

God, help us to win in our struggles,
and answer us when we call out to you.

Psalm  God, you help things work out for the best,
you are always on our side.
When we ask for help,
you respond with compassion,
giving us more than we could ever ask for.

Now,
destroy my enemies.

Devour them with fire.
Crush their evil schemes,
and shame them.

We rejoice because you always win.
We are happy that you are strong.

Psalm

God, you have deserted me,
and I am terrified.
Every minute of every day
I try to reach you,
but you are still nowhere to be found.

You have always been a good God,
and when we trusted you,
you came through for us.

But now
I feel like a slug.
Everyone
shoves me around
and puts me down, saying:
"You're stupid.
You believe God will help you.
But where's God now?"

But you have taken care of me
ever since I was born.
So, please, stay close to me now.
I need you.
It feels as though danger
is creeping up on me.
My heart feels broken,
my voice is weak,
and I feel harm is
just around the corner.
I feel that I am being picked apart,
that I am being busted wide open,
left high and dry.

God,
stay with me,
heal my pain.

I know you are listening.
I will tell others about you,
and I will always sing and dance
when I think of you.

All of you who truly believe in God,
do not forget to be thankful.
Remember now
that God never abandons us
when we are hurting;
God always listens to us.

Remember, and give thanks to God.
I don't know about the rest of you,
but I will live my life for God
and do what is right,
remembering
that God holds the answers.

Psalm

You are my shepherd,
why should I need anything or anyone else?
You help me to stay calm and steady,
you help me to find a gentle stream
where I feel refreshed
and renewed.

You make sure I stay
on the right road,
and you live up
to what everyone says about you.
Even when I feel
I am sinking into the worst,
I am not afraid,
because you are here with me.

You set a table for me,
providing all that I need,
and others who would
want to hurt me
have to watch from a distance,
frustrated.

You anoint me and heal me,
and I overflow with joy.

Every day I will come to know
your goodness and kindness.
I will live with you forever.

Psalm  The entire earth,
the whole world,
belongs to God—
every living thing,
every person,
every animal,
every plant and creature
are under God's protection.

Who has the skill
to climb God's mountain?
Only those who stay true
to the rule of God.
God will then bless them
and will allow them to see.

Keep the path open
for God to enter.

Who is this God of ours?
God is the one
who paves the way
for all that is right and good,
who keeps things clear
when everything seems
confused and blurred.

Who is this one who rules?
It is God:
Strong.
Loving.
Just.
Wise.
Holy.

Psalm

God,
I give everything to you.
If I trust you,
you will always come through.
If I do not,
I will be lost.

Help me to hear
everything clearly from you.
Teach me well,
and head me in the right direction,
for you are the only
way that makes sense.

Remember how tender
you can be.
Forget the times
that I have failed—
remember my best times.

You are so good, God.
You always help those
who feel lost.
Those who are poor
always know
that you are with them.

If we stay true to you,
you will be there for us.
Be a God that we can count on!
Forgive us as you have promised.

If we truly honor God,
then God will be there
in all our decisions.
We will be happy,
and we will know the favor
that only God can give.

When I am feeling trapped,
I look to God to rescue me.
Come now, God—
I need you more than ever.

Take away my pain,
and free me
from the trap I am in now.
Everyone seems to hate me.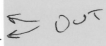

Take care of me;
I am leaning on you now.
I trust in your friendship.

 God,
I have tried to stay
on the right path;
I have tried to trust you.
So, come and help me!

Your love is everywhere I look,
and so I can be confident and strong.
I will not associate
with those who lie,
with those who say one thing
and do another.
I will not make bad choices.

I feel good about the choices I make
because they are your choices.
So I feel free,
ready to celebrate your presence.
God, I love being in your presence!

Do not ever let me fall backwards
and join the ways of those
who reject you.

I promise to stay on the right road,
to be honest.
I will keep my commitment to you,
always thanking you
for giving me strength.

Psalm

God is my light;
God shines bright when I am afraid.
God is the strong foundation
for my life—
how could I possibly be depressed
or fearful?

Because of God's light
watching over me,
no one can destroy me.
They constantly fail.
When they come to destroy me,
they collapse.
I will never be afraid.

I do not need much;
I only ask for one thing:
to be with you, God, always,
and to stay where you stay.

With you, God,
I will remain safe.
Those who want to hurt me
will not be able to reach me.
So, I will sing and honor you, my God.

God,
listen to me.
Show me your face,
do not stay far from me.
Try not to be angry with me,
but help me.

Even if my parents
or my dearest friends abandon me,
God will never abandon me.

God, show me how
I should live my life.
Keep me from slipping
into danger.

I am convinced that one day
I will see you, God,
face-to-face.

So keep trusting,
remain strong,
stay brave.
Trust God!

Psalm

I am calling on you, God.
Do not be deaf,
do not be silent.
I need you—
there is no other hope for me.

I need your mercy
and forgiveness;
I am reaching out to you.

Do not treat me badly,
like those who constantly
choose to do wrong.
Give them what they deserve,
because it is obvious
that they do not care about you.

Blessed are you, God,
for you do hear me.
You give me what I need.

When you help me,
I feel happy,
and so I will sing for you.

Keep us safe in your care,
always.

Psalm

Give everything you have
to God!
Thank God!
Honor God!
When you hear the name of God,
be humble.

God's voice is huge,
loud and strong!
God's voice can be heard
above all other voices.
God shatters anything
that gets in the way.

God's voice flames forth,
blazing through all
that would block the path.

Everyone in your house, God,
sings loudly and happily!
You are in charge of everything,
you are in charge!

Give us the strength that we need,
and fill us all with peace.

Psalm  God,
you deserve all the praise
that comes your way,
for you always are there for me.
I pleaded and begged you
to come to me,
and you did.
You have healed me.

I would ask everyone
to praise this awesome God of ours,
who never stays angry for long,
whose forgiving ways never pass,
and who always delights in us
and remains on our side.

When I am right with God,
everything goes well for me.
With God at my side,
I become strong and confident.
When God seems far away,
I am really afraid!

God,
please come back to me quickly!

Listen to me now,
help me!

You take my fear and trembling
and turn it into joy and music;
you lift me up from my sorrow
and give me reason for joy.

Open my mouth in praise;
help me to thank you,
always!

Psalm

I feel shame, God,
help me,
I am drowning.
I cannot seem to save myself;
I need you badly!
Be the strength that I need now.

Prove to me
that you really are God.
Pull me out of this.
I place my problems in your hands,
confident that you will respond.

I hurt all over,
my eyes are tired,
I ache everywhere.
I am consumed by all the things
that keep me afraid.
My energy is spent.

I feel the ridicule of others
all around me;
people avoid me.
I feel alone and forgotten,
broken in two,
attacked from every direction.

But I believe in you, God,
and hand over my problems to you.
Save me, please.
Look at me, and love me.
Get me out of this!

Keep the negative and taunting voices
far away from me;
surround me only with
what is good.
You are good to those who trust you.
You are generous
when we seek your help.

Blessed are you, God!
Your love is all around me.
I was too quick to feel as though
you were not there.
You have always been there,
always answered me when I needed you.

Listen, everyone,
love God!
If you wait for God,
stand firm and believe.

Psalm We should all be happy
when God forgives us,
washes away all that we have done
that keeps us in sin.

When I try to hide my wrongdoing,
I am weak.
I feel the weight of my sin,
I feel alone and isolated.

When I stop the hiding
and speak the truth,
I can ask for forgiveness
and feel God's peaceful love for me.

God,
no wonder we come to you
when we are in trouble!
You are the only one who
can help us during the hard times.

You keep telling us:
"Pay attention,
listen to me;
I will show you the way.
Don't worry,
I will look out for you.
Stop trying to be God;
I will be God."

When we sin, we only know sadness.
When we trust God, we know love.

Be happy with God.
Be glad!

Psalm  You are justice for everyone,
and so
we must praise you,
sing songs,
dance!

Your word is perfect,
it is always true;
what you say—you do.
Your love is unending;
it cannot be stopped.

When you speak,
heavens are created.
When you breathe in and out,
the stars find their way into the sky.
You keep the well full of living water.

We are completely astounded
by how awesome you are!
When you raise your voice,
things start to happen.

You are stronger
than any group of people;
you can turn upside down
the most well conceived plans.

Your plan is eternal,
and you bless this earth
where we dwell
because we are your chosen people.

You look down
and see all of us.
You know what is in our mind,
you know what we are thinking,
you know all our actions.

You change our way of thinking:
armies, force, and violence
cannot change things for the better.
Thugs, dictators, and hoods
are kidding themselves.

You keep loving us.
You watch our every move.
You keep us from falling into death.

With everything that we have,
with all our energy and effort,
we will be patient and wait for you.
It is in you that we find happiness,
and we trust you.
Keep loving us, God!
We can hardly wait to see you.

Psalm

There is absolutely no way
that I can ever stop thanking God.
Every part of me
is proud to follow God,
and all who are poor,
all who are hurting
will hear and rejoice with me!

Join me, everyone!
Let us go everywhere together
and tell people about God.
God has answered both you and me
and kept us in the clear.

When in doubt, turn to God,
and be happy.
God sends angels to us
to keep us safe.
Take it all in.
Taste it to the last portion,
and enjoy how wonderful
is the love of God.

God is awesome, let us not forget.
God will take care of us.

Listen to God,
listen well.
Do we really want to live well?

Stop speaking badly of people—
let others tell lies.
Walk away from evil,
seek to do good,
focus on the positive.

God will handle those
who cause harm.
God will come to us
if we are decent and good to others.
God will listen to our cries.

When we are in trouble—God listens.
God always spends time
with those who are discouraged.
When it seems we are going
through difficult times,
God will be with us,
protecting us each step of the way.

Evil will only end up being evil.
God will save us
when we stay faithful.

Psalm  **G**od,
give me the armor I need
to fight off those who are after me.

Tell me what I need to hear—
that you will protect me.
Drive away those who would hurt me.

Make your way known to them—
that harming others is wrong.
Teach them a lesson
they'll never forget.
Catch them in the same traps
they would use on others.

When you help me to be victorious,
I feel your presence.
God, there is no one quite like you.

When I fall down, my enemies cheer!
But you do not cheer, rather,
you pick me up and attend to my pain.

Do not stay silent;
take up my cause!

Do not let evil have the last word with me;
help me to see beyond that.
Bring me together with my friends,
and let them celebrate with me
in praising and thanking you.
God, you are so great in love!

Psalm  **S**ome people stink of evil.
They run from everything
that is good and right in the world.
They wear their sin
like a badge of honor.
They constantly lie,
they strategize to harm others.

Your mercy is hard to describe—
there is nothing quite like it!

It is amazing! It is everywhere!
Your fairness to all is seen by everyone,
and you are so wise,
you never run out
of the right way to lead us.
You embrace everything that is good;
how fortunate we are to have you!

People everywhere seek your help
and want to be held by you.
They come to you,
and you quench their thirst.
You give all of us living water.
You are a fountain
that never goes dry.
You are a light for all to see.

Don't retreat from us;
remain merciful and kind,
defend us when we need you.

Psalm  We should try to not worry so much
about those who make bad choices,
about those who seem to seek harm.
They will not last long.

We should focus more on God,
on trusting God.
We should calm down
and be more at peace with things.
We should spend more time
remembering how wonderful
God is with us.

We need to offer everything
over to God,
and be confident
that God will do what is right for us.

Be still for a moment,
wait for God, listen to God.

Stop spending so much time
worrying about those
who scheme against you.
It will only eat you alive.

Again, remember,
God will take care of them.
We only have to wait for God,
and we will receive plenty.

People who destroy, murder, steal, rape
will be hurled off the face of the earth.
Evil people waste their energy
on equally evil schemes,
hoping that God won't find out.
But God knows everything,
and has plans for them.
They will fall into their own traps.
Their plots will collapse.

But God will support us if we choose rightly,
for God has always been there
for those who live well
and who ask God for help in their life.

God will be there in the hard times;
we will never go hungry.
Those who oppose God will lose,
for they always take and take
and never give anything back.

Those who give
without expectation of return,
God will treat well.
God is happy with us when we choose well;
if we fall, God will pick us up
and help us to move forward again.

Throughout my entire life
I have never seen God abandon those
who are in need.
God is good—always.

Abandon bad choices,
and you will receive a blessing
beyond measure.

When we are right with God,
we will never fail.
We will find knowledge and wisdom.

We need to have hope
that God will give us
the strength that we need.
Stay honest and good,
and the future will be ours.
If we choose violence and harm,
we will be lost.

Psalm Please do not punish me, God,
or crush me with your anger.
When you are angry,
I shake all over.
When I sin,
I feel weak and fearful,
weighted down
by the stupid choices I have made.
I am getting what I deserve.

I feel miserable;
all day long I can't seem to shake it.
Sick to my stomach,
my heart is broken.

God, you know what I long for,
you know all the things
that I am afraid of.
My heart is beating fast and wild,
and I am feeling dizzy in my fear.

My friends keep their distance.
My enemies plot my failure.
I cannot speak, I can't hear,
I have nothing to say
to defend my actions.
But I will wait to listen
to what you have to say.

I know I have done wrong,
and I am sorry.

Some seem to hate me
for no reason at all,
blaming me because
I try to do the right thing.

Please don't leave me, God!
Hurry.

Psalm 39

I told everyone
that I would not make this mistake,
that I would not screw up,
not make the wrong choice.
I will keep my mouth zipped shut
when they come after me.
Yet, fear came over me,
and I gave in to it,
and the words came spilling out.

God, what will happen now?
Is my life over?

I know that every day is a gift.
I know that they mean little
when compared to you.
Our individual life is but a speck,
insignificant,
amounting to nothing.

Sometimes I wonder—
why do I wait
and place my hope in you?
But I know deep down that
you are the only hope for me.

Stop torturing me;
when you come after me, I feel it.
You confront us when we sin,
and we have to face the consequences.

I am praying to you, God,
hear me.
Don't reject me,
listen to me when I cry.

Please let me know
that I can be happy again.

Psalm 40

I waited
and I waited for God.
Finally,
God came and heard my concerns,
pulled me out of my fear,
and gave me steady feet
to keep walking,
to keep moving on.

God, put a new song in my heart,
a song that can be given to everyone
who trusts in God.

We are happy
when we have faith in God,
and we cannot be influenced by others,
only by God,
God alone.

God,
you do so many things
that show us how much
you really do love us.
God, you are so awesome!
The list of your great deeds
goes on and on!

You do not want me
to offer a sacrifice;
you only ask me to be attentive
and to listen well.

So I will listen to what you say—
I will live by the rules
that you have placed within me.
I want to do what you want,
for your teaching is the best.

I celebrate with everyone
how good and fair you are!

I will not be sheepish,
I will not hold back;
I will share it with everyone.
You know I will.

I will not keep hidden
the fantastic things you have done.
Everyone will hear the story!

Evil seems to be everywhere;
sometimes my sins are overwhelming,
and I lose heart.
God, help me,
keep me out of harm's way.

Remember us when we seek you,
strengthen us when we need you,
help us to sing when the voice seems silent,
give us the songs to sing!

Even though I feel weak and poor,
I know God is always with me.
God—come now!

Psalm  The ones who reach out
to the poor,
the less fortunate—
they are blessed by God.

God watches out for them
and fills them with blessings.
When they are sick,
God brings them back to health.

I have cried out to God, saying:
"God, I need you.
Forgive and heal me,
for I know I have let you down."
Those who hate me, well,
they wish the worst for me.
They secretly hope
that I will not get better.

Even my best friend,
who I thought was so good to me,
is now against me.

God, bring me back to health.
Then I will know
that you are at my side.
Let me be with you always.

Bless you, God!
Always!

Psalms  Like a thirsting deer,
I need you badly, God.
I am thirsting for you.
You are living water.
When can I be with you?

I am in agony.
All around me voices say,
"Where is God?"

I remember when things were better,
when I felt close to you,
when I was at home with you.

Why am I so sad?
Must I wait for God?

The sea of fears, worries, nightmares
overwhelms and drowns me.
I call upon the love of God.
I complain:
"God, where are you—
have you forgotten me?"

Why am I so sad?
Must I wait for God?

I need you on my side,
defend me.
I need you to be strong for me.
Again, I am asking,
Have you forgotten me?

Give me insight,
and tell me the truth.
With these things
I can find my way to you—
you, the joy of my life.
I will praise you forever.

Why am I so sad?
I will wait for you, my God.
And I will always praise you.

Psalm  I have heard about you,
about all the wonderful things
you have done.
I have heard the story
about how you turned things
upside down
and took care of those you loved.

It was you, God,
it was you who brought them to freedom.
It was you, and is you,
who keeps us safe from our enemies,
protected from harm.
We never cease to praise you.

So why do you leave us
open for defeat?
Why do we feel like sheep
ready to be slaughtered?
People come and laugh at us,
making us the butt of their jokes.
They joke about our honesty
and sneer at our hopes.
We feel embarrassed
by their teasing and their cruelty.

We endure,
and we have not abandoned you,
but at times
we feel that you have abandoned us.

48

Please, God,
wake up and be with us now!
Why are you silent?
Why do you ignore us when we need you?

We are hanging on by a thread,
so help us. Now.

Psalm  I am filled with a song right now,
a song that I have to sing.
God has blessed you,
so show justice and care for the poor,
use your power wisely, and be strong.
Fairness should be the center
of all that you do.

Forget the things that you once held dear,
and seek the One who cares for you.
Your children will inherit
all the good things
you and your parents once had.

Your name will always be remembered;
the song will go on forever!

Psalm  We can always be sure of
God, and God alone.
God will always watch out for us.
No matter how harsh the disaster—
families torn apart,
losses and failures,
betrayal by friends—
God will be there to lift us up.

God's power is large,
always protecting us.

The Reign of God is surrounded
by a river of joy,
and God will always defend it.

Nations and armies
brag and swagger,
but they fall on their own sword.
Even when God speaks softly,
change happens,
things begin to quiver.

God's power is large,
always protecting us.

Come and see
all these awesome things!
Wars are ended,
all because of God!
Stop your fighting,
and look to God.

God's power is large,
always protecting us.

Psalm  Everyone!
Clap, sing, dance!
Make sure God can hear
the joy you feel!
God is awesome,
greater than anything else!

God sets us free
and gives us a land to delight in.

God climbs the mountain
to cheers and applause!
Give a cheer for God!

For God watches,
taking care of everyone and everything!
God is in charge!
From near and far,
everything in sight
and everything not seen—
everything belongs to God!

Psalm

God is deserving
of every praise we can offer.
Everything is beautiful
because of God!

Those who try to destroy
the beauty of creation
retreat in the knowledge
that they cannot win.

What we have experienced
is what we have always been promised.
God's world is a wonderful
and beautiful place,
a place of love.

God,
your glory fills the entire world.
Your ways always win out,
and we rejoice.

Everyone,
sing and rejoice:
God is here!
God will never leave us!
God will save us from death!

Psalm

Pay careful attention!
I want all of you to listen,
because I have something
that you need to hear.
I can see clearly now;
I have stayed focused.

It is amazing to me
that I can be afraid of my enemies
with God at my side.

We cannot save ourselves,
only God can save us.
No matter how hard we try,
we cannot achieve
what God alone can do.

We try to avoid pain and death,
but it is impossible to escape.
Even the most wise,
the wealthiest,
and the healthiest—
finally all die.

No matter how great we think we are,
we all die the same.
But our destiny is not the same.
For those who only care about themselves—
they will be lost forever.

But we know that God will keep us safe,
even when we die.
There is a wonderful place waiting for us.

Don't be concerned about money
when it seems that someone else
has more wealth than you do.
It will all mean nothing when we die.

The truth is the same for all of us—
someday we will all die.
Life is priceless.

Psalm  God is greater
than any other God
we could imagine or manufacture.
God calls all creation
from every end of the earth,
and the beauty God gives
is awesome!

God will not stay quiet
but will become known
through the forces of fire and storm,
and will offer testimony for us:

"Listen, everyone,
hear my words—
I come to judge you.
I have no need for your sacrifices,
for I own everything to begin with.

Stop sacrificing things,
and start giving thanks,
be grateful.
When you are in trouble,
call out to me.
I will come through for you,
and then you should sing praises."

God says to those who choose badly:
"Stop telling me what I have commanded,
for you go against my laws and commands.
You speak badly of others,
you lie to your own family—
I know how you act.
I bring my case against you now,
so think about these things,
reflect deeply on what happens
when you ignore me."

If we are thankful, God will honor our life.
If we follow God, we will be happy forever.

Psalm  Forgive me, God,
have mercy.
Try to forget that I have sinned.
Purify me from
the evil that I have done.
I know what I have done;
I cannot escape it,
it follows me everywhere.

You are right to punish me;
I truly deserve it.
You know me,
you know how I can be.
You have always known.

Your love is for those
who live honestly.
Teach me to be that way.
Wash me with fresh water.
Cleanse my soul
bright as the snow.

Put joyful songs into my voice
and into my heart.
Close your eyes to all the
awful things I have done.
Make them go away,
give me a new heart,
put a loving spirit in me.
Don't turn away from me.

Help me find joy again.
I need your support,
I need your strength.
If you give these to me,
I will invite others to follow you.
I need your help
to stop crying,
to start singing.

All I can offer to you is myself,
shattered, broken, human.
But changed, truly changed.
Hopefully this offering to you—
the greatest gift I can give—
will please you.

Psalm I don't understand—
why brag about doing wrong!
Why proudly announce
the evil things you have done?
I guess you value harm to others
over goodness and honesty.
You want to create a world
full of pain and suffering.
So you lie and slander,
spread false rumors, and
generally talk trash.

God will punish you;
you will have to face the music
because you trusted in money,
drowned yourself in materialism,

manipulated people,
and relished wrongdoing.
You foolishly depended
on your childish attempts at power
rather than leaning on God.

Like a budding tree
nourished by God's grace,
I am growing strong and tall
in God's garden.
I trust in God.
God, thank you
for all that you do for me.
I always give credit to you
when others ask me
about my good fortune.

Psalm  The foolish say
that there is no God.
It gives them an excuse
to make bad decisions
and to lead a lousy life.

God watches those who are wise.
True wisdom means
that we rely on God.

But at times
our entire world seems corrupt,
and it seems that goodness
cannot be found anywhere.
Have we all gone crazy?
God wonders sometimes.
It seems as though we never pray,
never show kindness or justice to others.

We need to be shaken up
and to remember that God will judge us.
We need to let God rule over our life
and restore us to health.
Then we will have something
to sing about.

Psalm 54

God,
I am hoping
that you will be there for me,
so listen to me now.
It seems that lots of people
are suddenly against me,
as if they want me to die.
I wish I had wings and
could fly away from all this
like an eagle.

But you will uphold me,
I really believe that.
Let them try,
let them make their plots
and try to knock me down.
I know they won't win.
You will give them
what they deserve.
For every lie they tell,
may each one come back to haunt them.
Twist their tongues;
strike them speechless.

I will give everything to you—
my entire life.
You are my Friend forever,
my constant Companion.
And I will praise you,
for you saved me from
those who want to hurt me.

Psalm 55

God,
please listen to me.
Don't walk away,
stay with me and listen.

My life is hard;
sometimes I think
I'm going insane.

Everyone is against me,
ganging up
and abusing me.
I can't take it anymore;
my anxiety keeps growing.

If I had wings,
I would fly far away from it all,
just to escape the tension.
Everywhere I look
I see hurt and pain,
violence and prejudice;
it seems never to stop.

But I will take my fear
and let you take it away from me.
I give it to you,
and I believe that you can make me whole again.
I have always been able to talk to you,
so don't let me down now.

I call out to you—
when I awake,
when I go to bed at night—
constantly begging you.
I know you hear me,
especially when things are
rough like this.
Everyone else in my life
breaks their promises;
not you—never.
You always are there.
I can give to you my burdens,
and you will support me.

Those who do not look to you,
they will lose, big time.
But I will trust you,
and I will find joy.

Psalm

It is time for your mercy
to show up.
I need it now.
Things are desperate.
I feel surrounded by evil,
and I need you.

When I am afraid,
I look to you.
I trust in your word.
With that being the case,
how can I lose?

Those who hate me
never let up.
They continually try to trip me up,
they wait for me to mess up.
Show them how angry you are, God!
You know how I am suffering,
so let's see some action.
For I am sure of one thing:
You are on my side,
you want me to be happy.

I will keep my promises to you, God,
because, once again, you
have saved me from harm
and kept me from drowning
in my fears, worries, and failures.
I will follow you,
for your light is brighter
than any other force.

Psalm

I need you to care for me.
I have no place else to go.
Stay with me
until I feel safe.
You are my hero,
and I need you to come now
and rid me of those
who want to hurt me.

Your love never leaves,
and I am glad,
because right now I feel
very much afraid.
I feel the walls closing in,
like if I take one wrong step,
I'll fall into a deep pit.

God, release your power!
Let your ways be seen by everyone!
They are trying to trick me,
but, instead,
they are falling into their own trap.

I have finally come to a decision:
I will only praise you!
I will dust off the trumpet
or guitar or piano or drums,
and start playing for you,
singing of your love,
always there,
never pulling away from me!
God, release your power!
Let your ways be seen by everyone!

Psalm  All of you who claim to be a god,
are you fair in your ways?
No way!
You choose selfishness and violence
to solve problems.
From the very beginning
you have been liars.
Like cobras
you spit poison in all your words.
You are deadly.

God, crush these snakes,
that they may turn to ooze
like a salted snail.
Stop them,
rob them of power,
sweep them away!

You are judge.
Do your work
so we can live in the way of right
and have a life of peace.

Psalm **G**od,
they are coming after me.
Raise me above their anger.
Come and rescue me.
Come now,
show up quickly,
and keep me far away from them—
bring me to safety.

They come out of nowhere,
they snicker and haunt me:
"Who will listen to you?
Nobody cares about you!"

You, God, care.
You laugh at their
silly attempts to make trouble.
I am watching for you, God.
I know you are compassionate,
so do not kill them,
but weaken their desire to hurt me and others.
Humble them,
so they can see how they are losers.
Then, maybe, they can find
their way to you.

I am awed by your strength,
and every day I am thankful that you love me.
You make me want to sing,
for you love me
and care for me.
I am free!

Psalm

I feel rejected by you, God.
You have turned away.
I am almost starting to believe
that you want us to suffer,
to feel hopeless and sad.

Instead, take our side,
help us count on you for strength.
Reach out to us,
and we will reach out to you.
When you hold on tight to us,
we can get through anything.

Psalm

I am so discouraged, God,
it is hard to stay confident.
I need you to restore my hope.
Bring me back to your house,
help me to feel your embrace.
I know you hear me;
bless me.

Be with me forever
so I can feel secure.
I will sing to you, God,
and keep my promises.

Psalm

Body and soul,
I am waiting quietly for God.
God is my strong foundation,
and in God I feel safe.

Some of you are relentless
in attacking others.
How much longer
will you continue?
You do not believe in love,
you only believe in death and suffering.

So I wait for God,
quietly, silently.
God is my strong foundation,
and in God I feel safe.
I advise all of you,
give your heart,
give your life to God!
God will not disappoint.

Our status—rich or poor—
has no lasting importance.
So be careful,
avoid being dishonest,
don't put your heart in wealth—
it will give you nothing lasting.
Over and over again,
God keeps telling us:
"Stop looking for security elsewhere;
look only to me.
My love will be the only strength you need."

Psalm  God, I ache for you.
Let me see you,
let me see who you are
and the things you do.

Your love is better than anything else.
I can't help but keep talking
about your goodness.
My whole life will be a reflection
of your glory,
and I reach out to you;
feasting upon your nourishment,
I will always be thankful.

As I drift calmly off to sleep at night,
I remember your blessings and gifts.
Gratitude fills my soul.
You have always helped me;
I am thankful.
I want to stay close to you,
for you help me to feel whole.

Psalm  4

Guard me, God,
I need protection.
Everyone seems to be
sharpening their sword
against me,
and their nasty words
pierce me even deeper.
How can people be so hateful?
They wallow in stupidity,
laughing, "We're so sharp,
nobody knows what we're doing."

I know that you will see to it
that they will fall on their own sword,
that their words will come back
to haunt them.
You are so awesome and wonderful, God!
In you we are protected,
you take such steady and sure care of us!

Psalm 65

Now is the time, creator God,
to give back to you
what you have given to us.
You liberate us
from the prison of our guilt,
and we are free from our pain.
You inspire us,
and give us so much to believe in.
You keep things steady;
you still the raging storms
of fear and anger, worry and stress
that well up within us.
You keep things fresh,
alive, and new.

You continually shower
gifts and blessings
too many to count!
The fields are filled with crops.
The sun shines and rain falls.

Bright flowers dazzle!
Our hearts are filled with joy!
We can't stop singing!

Psalm Everyone, all the earth,
praises you, God of all creation,
and we should, too!
You are awesome,
everything you do is stupendous!
Because of your strength,
armies stand down,
and the beauty of creation buds forth,
singing about you!

Come, everyone,
and see the tremendous things
our God has done!
Miracles!
Seas turn to dry land,
and those seeking freedom
cross over to new life.
Keep praising God;
let no one who seeks harm
find their way to us.
Get the news out:
God has brought us relief
from our worst selves,
and from those forces that wish us dead.
God promises good things for us,
and God delivers.

Psalm  Shine your light on us, God.
Let everyone see how good you are.
The people will be joyous
when they experience you firsthand.
You astound us all
with your justice and fairness.
Your creation sustains our life.

Everyone will be joyous.
God, keep blessing us,
and we will praise you always.

Psalm

When God is with us,
all evil vanishes.
Faced with God,
hate, envy, greed, and brutality
melt like candle wax,
blow away
like leaves in a windstorm.

But we who are faithful to God,
we are happy,
and we celebrate!
Sing songs, make merry,
start the music and dance.
God has many wonderful names;
sing them all!
Defender, Protector,
Loving Parent for us!
Liberator! The Merciful!
Holy Friend!

If we are homeless,
God finds us a new place to live.
Prisoners are set free,
but destroyers and thieves
are kept behind locked doors.
Those who worship their possessions
are possessed by them instead.
But when you led people to new land,
the earth moved
and the rains came.
You keep repeating yourself;
the rain keeps coming,
nourishing all that lives
and giving strength to those
who need new confidence.
When you speak,
good things happen.

We should never stop
blessing God,
who keeps us alive,
who maintains our safety.
As you have always done in the past,
give us your strength now, God.
Keep us safe from those who hate us.
We remember that you are God,
you are in charge,
you are the force to guide our life.
Keep inspiring us,
fill us with your power.
Bless you, God!

Psalm

I am drowning fast, God.
I am sinking
with no ledge to grab on to.
I keep shouting,
and no one seems to hear me.
I strain to find you,
and I am blinded by your absence.
It seems I am alone
with only those who hate me.
They keep accusing me
of things I have not done.

God, you know me,
you know the truth.
They attack me because
I believe in you.
I have lost friends
because of my faith in you.
Believing in you
has had its cost and taken its toll.
All I seem to have is
ridicule from them all.
I am teased;
they make fun of me.

Send your help, hear me,
I am praying to you.
Take my arms,
I will hang on tight
and look into your eyes
as you lift me up.
What are you waiting for?
Now is the time,
you know what I am feeling,
I feel embarrassed—
and they are taking advantage.

I feel sick.
Heal me, God,
heal me.
I will then thank you
with all my heart.
You free all who suffer.
You give us new hope when we're hopeless,
food when we hunger,
and freedom when we feel the chains.
I praise you, God!

Psalm Help me.
Please help me.
I feel so alone, so unloved.
I do not understand why people
want me to fail.
I am reaching out to you
because I believe that you love me.
You are great and loving,
so come now.
I am poor and empty.
Hurry, God,
hurry.

Psalm 71

You, God, are the protective wall
that I always need.
You will never fail me
or see me shamed.
I need to be able to turn to you,
for I cannot trust anyone else.
You are all I have.

Ever since I was a young child,
I have felt you near me.
I have always relied on you;
from the time I was born,
you were there.
When I have felt isolated,
you were always there.
So now that I am older,
don't forget to be with me.

Don't be stingy with your love,
fill me deeply.
Drive off those who seem
to enjoy my suffering.
I will try to not lose hope,
and I will always be thankful.
It is impossible to recall
all the good things you have done for me.
Don't stop now.

Even though I have to suffer sometimes,
you always come to the rescue.
You are a true friend to me, God.
How wonderful you are!
I will stand tall
and tell everyone I can about you!

Psalm 72

God,
give us the gifts that we need;
help us to be just as you are just,
compassionate as you are compassionate.
You are a fair God,
and that fairness you make known to us
time and time again.

May our leaders learn your lessons
and help us build a world
of justice, compassion, and peace.
Then, the poor will no longer be shamed,
those who are alone will have an abundance
of friends and blessings.
Your mercy will surround us.

I love your name, God,
and I will make it be known to everyone!
You keep blessing us,
and we keep singing!

Psalm When we do the right thing,
you are good to us!
But we too often imitate
or at least try to imitate
those who are rich,
those with just the right body,
the arrogant and proud.
This mistake is easy.
We are tempted to think
that some never stumble.
As I watch them,
it seems as though they do everything right.

But then the covering of their illusion
begins to fall apart—
they make choices that
are against your will,
and they choose to sin.
They think that they are in control,
and, unfortunately,
many people believe
and follow them.
They pull many away from you,
and many weaken
and follow them blindly.
It would be easy to be like them,
but then I would be betraying you,
and betraying the people whom you love.

After a while their tactics
catch up with them.
So I stay close to you,
and you reach out
and take me by your hand.
I want to learn your ways, God.
I need to remember
that all I need is you.
If I lose my money,
if I cannot run the fastest
or buy the latest things,
it should not matter,
because you will be there for me.
Being near you—this makes me happy.
This is being smart,
and I will share this good news.

Psalm 74

Why are you ignoring me?
God, why have you forgotten me?
In the past you have always
remembered your people;
do not forget us now.
Yes, people sneer at religion.
Yes, violent crime claims
more and more lives,
especially young people.
Yes, we act irresponsibly,
polluting the earth.
But do not abandon us
to ourselves.
In the midst of all the pain
that is going on around me,
I hear no word from you,
no sign, no voice—
where are you?

God, you have always been in charge,
you have always saved us
when we have needed you.
You are at the center of all things,
so do not forget.

Remember!
Do not leave your poor ones alone.
In one way or another,
we are all poor.
Remember,
you promised.
You promised to be there
during these times of trial.
Come now,
do what you do so well!
Don't be silent!

Psalm Thanks to you, generous God,
you are here with us.
You always speak with wisdom.
We listen to your voice:
"I will decide when to act;
I will set things right.
Those of you who are arrogant,
stop your boasting,
stop showing off."

Only you, God, can judge.
You alone decide.
You decide who will receive reward
and who will go away emptyhanded.

Thank you, God,
the one who keeps the proud humble
and the humble proud.

Psalm God,
everyone knows who you are.
Everyone knows how powerful you are!
When you strike,
no one can fight back
no matter how hard they try.
No one can battle you, God.
We should not even try.

Your voice is stronger and louder
than any other sound.
You are the judge
who defends those who have no defense.

So listen, all of you—
keep your promises to God.

Psalm 77

God, every day I cry,
every night I pray to you,
but it seems as though
you refuse to listen.
I cannot sleep,
I am deeply troubled.
Will God always be silent to me?
Has God stopped loving me?

I am scared to think that maybe
God is no longer the strength
that I thought I had.
I keep remembering
all the amazing things
that God has done before.
God, you are God,
I want to believe that.
You have always shown your power,
you have always reached out to
those who suffer.
You made the oceans rise,
and used your thunder and rain
to send a message.
The message always got through.
You have always made a clear path.
You have led us always to the right place.
Lead on again, my God.

Psalm

Friends,
let me begin with a story,
an old story
that has been shared
and passed down
from generation to generation.
We must remember
to share this story with everyone we can.
God has taken care of us always,
and that message must continue.
Let your friends and children learn
that God can be trusted,
that God's way is the only way.

Many people in the past forgot
the great deeds of God—
and they stumbled through life, lost.
God parted the sea,
and the Israelites were able to escape
through it all.
During the day, bright clouds guided them;
at night, a pillar of fire for light.

When the people were thirsty,
God opened up the rocks,
and fresh water flowed!
Yet, God's actions did not impress them,
for they did not reform their lives.
They tried to test God;
even so God remained faithful.
In the midst of their hunger and doubt,
God sent them bread,
and showered it upon them all.
They had more than they needed.
But that still was not enough for them.
They ate and they ate,
and finally God became angry,
striking down many of them.

But still they didn't see.
Their lives were miserable,
and they ended without joy,
without promise.

Some tried to change,
and they cried out to God,
but God saw through the lies.

Yet, God was loving and compassionate,
forgiving them.
God remembered that they were human.
Often they were rebellious
and tried to blame God,
but they forgot that God was loving.
So God sent them signs,
plagues, times of pain and destruction,
and none survived.
Those who trusted God
were kept safe through it all,
while the others drowned in the sea.

The People of God were led to a wonderful new place,
God's home.
But they still did not seem to understand,
and they continued to test God,
and they began to follow the ways of other gods,
and they abandoned the God who loved them.
God then kept them at a distance,
and finally sent them a servant named David.
It was David's task to help
bring them back home.
So David led them with care, but firmly.
Once again God stayed faithful,
even though the people
failed and were faithless.

Psalm   God,
we build bigger and more destructive bombs,
we pollute your creation with noxious fumes,
we shoot one another with automatic weapons,
we fry our brain with drugs.
Is it any wonder that you grow weary of us?
Please don't stay angry for long.

Make your displeasure known,
but, please, don't blame us for mistakes
that others made before us.
Be loving.
Forgive us when we make mistakes.
Don't let others destroy what you have built.
Give us the grace to do better,
to build the earth.
We are your people,
and we will always remember that.
We thank and praise you, creator God.

Psalm   Hear us,
shepherd us, God.
See us for who we are.
If you are in heaven,
we need you here.
Take care of us now.
We need to be brought back to you.
So come now,
help us to change!
Save us from ourselves!

You are angry;
we have not paid attention,
and we have put all the blame on you.
So come now,
help us to change!
Save us from ourselves!

You have prepared the world for us,
nurtured it and us as well,
and many have destroyed
what you have planted.
Come back to us—
look at our situation here,
and give us another chance.
Help us to show once more
how we can cherish and value
all that you have given us.

Everything we have comes from you.
We have not turned away,
so do not turn away from us.
Bring us back to life—please.
If we can change, it is because of you.
So come now,
help us to change!
Save us from ourselves!

Psalm

Time to celebrate,
time to tell everyone about God!
Sing, dance, shout,
turn up the volume
so everyone can hear!
God has lifted all the burdens
from our back;
God keeps protecting us,
and comes rushing to our side
when we are hurting.

God wants us to remember
that we only need to reach out.
If we listen well,
God will give us the tools we need
to get us through
the mess that we find ourselves in.

But we forget to listen,
we think we can do it on our own.
Or we think that others
can save us from our troubles.
They can help,
but only God can truly
make things better for us.
God is so sad
because we don't reach out.
God wants us to be happy,
and will free us from our troubles.
All we have to do is reach out and listen,
and God will take care of the rest.

Psalm    God, you are in charge of everything.
You alone decide what will happen to us.

Do your work, God,
make it clear.
Those who are lonely will find friends.
The hungry will have enough to eat.
The weak will be strong.
Those who are victims
will regain their rights
and have good things done for them.
God, you alone are the judge.
All decisions for our future are in your hands.

Psalm    God,
I am waiting and waiting.
I am trying to be patient.
I am waiting for you to speak.
Say something!
Pay attention to what is going on.
Greedy, violent people
ravage your creation.

I wish you would fix things, God.
I wish you would bring them
all down to size.
They need a taste of their own medicine.
Bring them to their knees.
Make them hit bottom.
Confuse and confound
the bullies and abusers,
the scam artists and tyrants.
Then they may turn to you.
You alone are God,
and we should never forget that.

Psalm 84

There is nothing quite like
being with you.
When I have felt very close to you, God,
I knew what home was all about.
I can hardly wait to feel that way again.
Every part of me
wants to be with you again.
Even sparrows can find a home with you,
and so I, too, long to be with you.
You protect the weakest and the most capable.
You are safe shelter, true peace.
Being with you is the best there is,
and I thank you.

I would rather be with you
for just a few moments
than to spend hours or years
with anyone else.
I only want to be where you are.
Being with you is wonderful calm,
true contentment,
and joy beyond imagining.

Psalm 85

Forgiving God,
it is amazing to me
that you forgive me
over and over again.
You accept me for who I am.
God, bring us back to you
when we leave you.
Give us new energy,
energy to become one with you again.

You, God,
speak about peace,
peace for everyone who loves you.
You, God,
speak about a world
where everyone is good to one another,
where peace and justice are one and the same,
where love is everywhere,
and where promises are kept.

I see the good things that you send.
You help things to grow,
and only the good survives.

Psalm 86

I want to hear what you have to say, God.
I am trying to be good,
trying very hard to trust you
when things go crazy around me.
Please feel sorry for me, God.
Help me to feel happy again.
In the past you always forgave me,
always accepted me.

When I pray,
I need you to listen.
I need you to do something.
Everyone comes from all around
to share how good you are.
You do incredible things;
you are God!
Reveal the way you want me to walk,
help me to hear your voice.

I thank you in the best way
I know how.
You love me time and time again.
It is impossible to describe.
You, God,
you are wonderful and accepting,
you do not anger easily,
you love me even when it is hard
for me to love myself.
Be kind to me, please.
Send me a sign.

Psalm 87

Everyone is searching, God.
Everyone looks to you,
everyone seeks to know where you dwell.
There is no place like your home.
I have tried to find a place
that I can call home.
All of us are welcome with you.
I do not have to look very far,
my home is here—with you!

Psalm 88

No matter what time of day
it might be,
I am always looking for you, God.
So, please,
hear me out.
I am in trouble,
big trouble.
I need you
as I have never needed you before.
I feel alone and forgotten.
I feel as though
you have forgotten that I exist;
you seem to be punishing me.

You have taken away everything
that I love—my friends,
my sense of security.
Are you really a God who performs miracles?
Are you really a God who forgives?

Or is it that you just can't forgive me?
I really feel anger from you, God.
I feel alone,
really alone.
The dark is my only companion.

Psalm

My heart is filled with joy,
and I can't stop singing and celebrating,
for God loves me so much!
This love never ends;
there is nothing that I can do
to escape God's love.
How wonderful!
You have made promises to me,
you have chosen me,
and you are the one
whom I want to follow.

Everywhere I look
I see how you have touched
and affected things—
no one is like you!

You stir things up,
you calm things down;
you are everywhere,
you can do anything!
Everything that is beautiful
comes from you.
You give new meaning
to words like
"love,"
"faithfulness,"
and "justice."
Your power is unmatched,
and people who experience you
feel joy like they never have before.

I pledge my love to you,
and I promise you my best,
all that I can give.
You will not stop being faithful,
so I will not stop being faithful,
because in the midst of all the insanity,
you are the only thing
that makes sense.
You are the only constant
in a galaxy of confusion, of madness.

Please remain with us—
we need you.

You did not create me for nothing,
I am here to serve you.
And I will serve you
and bless you always.

Psalm Throughout all time,
among all things,
you have always been there.
To you, one day is nothing.
Thousands of years have gone by,
and for you
it is only a moment.

My life seems so short;
I try to live a day at a time,
sometimes one minute at a time.
You see the big picture, God.
My life is but a small morsel
of the feast that you have created.
So I need you to help me to live well.
Help me make the best use
of the life that I have.

I hope you will come again soon,
I need you.
Help us to be happy,
help us to be more loving.
Help us to count our blessings
while we go through these hard times.
Bless us,
guide us in all we do.

Psalm All of you who are in hiding,
all who are protected
in God's embrace,
call out to God,
"You are the one I need,
you are the one I trust."
God will take care of you
in the worst of times.

God will help you to find cover,
God will always protect you.

At nighttime you will no longer be afraid;
you will be able to dodge the problems
that come your way.
Nothing will harm you.
Many may drop and fall to pieces
on either side of you,
but you will be kept safe.
God will be with you.

Notice how God punishes
the wicked ones;
you have God's armor on your side,
you have protection.
You will never have anything to fear,
you can rest peacefully.
God sends angels, "ministers,"
to be with you on the way.
They will support you, pray for you,
and you will stay on the right path.

God tells us:
"I will save those who stay close to me,
be there for those who know me,
answer those who ask for help,
stand with all who are in trouble.
These are the ones I will always take care of,
and they will live a long life
and show everyone what I can do."

Psalm  It is a good thing
to give thanks to you,
to begin each day thanking you.
I try to remember that
throughout the entire day,
because there are so many reasons
to thank you.
You give us many reasons
to be happy.

I am amazed
at some of the things you do.
Many people do not understand
how wonderful you are.
In the midst of it all,
you remain constant.

We have to remember
that bad things seem to drift away
while you strengthen us.
I have seen these people
who I know want to hurt me,
but everything around me
continues to grow and remain vibrant.
It is a good thing
to give you thanks.

Psalm  God,
you rule all creation;
no one is greater than you!
Because of you
everything remains steady.
The ocean roars,
the thunder crashes,
all in praise of their Creator.
Your ways never end.

Psalm  God, you shake up those with power.
You tear down their arrogance
and put them in their place.
But why do these people always
seem to be around?
They murder innocent children,
victimize helpless elders.
They deprive the poor of food
and keep just wages from powerless workers.

And yet they seem to flourish
everywhere.
They think they can get away
with anything;
they believe that you are deaf
or just don't care.
They forget that you are God,
powerful and just!

So, God,
we need your blessing;
come and teach us the right way
to live and to treat one another.
Help us to be like you,
people who do not renege on promises;
help us to be people
peaceful to everyone we meet.

Without you
I would be dead by now.
When I feel I am beginning to mess up,
I feel you right behind and beside me,
ready to hold me upright.
When I worry too much,
you calm me down.
God, stay with me always,
help me when I feel unsafe,
and challenge those who choose badly
to see and repent of the consequences
of their actions.

Psalm

Come with me,
everyone!
Come with me
and sing loudly,
and come to know God.
God is great.
God holds everything close.
God shaped all creation
and dwells with us now.

Honor God,
and remember
that we are God's people.
God has chosen us,
and God will always take care of us.

If we have heard God's voice,
let us open our heart
to listen and take heed.

Psalm

Offer God a brand-new song!
Let everyone hear it,
let it go on forever!
God is unbelievable!
God is awesome!
God deserves to be praised,
for God made everything good
and keeps things new and fresh!

Everyone, everywhere!
Tell everyone about God!
Pray well and strong;
sing out, and never stop!
Make sure everyone knows
that God is in charge!
God is always right—
the first time.
God never has to recant.
Let everything—
sea and land,
sun and moon,
birds and fish—
and everyone give praise to God!

Amazing things will start to happen—
miracles will abound,
for God is here
to make things right
and to give life to the full.

Psalm

God, you rule the universe,
and we are glad!
You guide us with justice and wisdom.
Come, God, show us
new possibilities.
Your fiery love
burns away hatred.
When it comes near,
all that is evil runs the other way.
If you command it, mountains will fall,
and you can show us
things we never thought were possible!

Everyone evil should stay
out of God's way—
let God do what God will do
so everyone can see.
God, you do unbelievable things,
more than we could ever imagine.
If we love you,
then we hate all that is violent,
selfish, and negative.
You will keep us safe.
Rain will come to
bring new life to those who are fair.
You send light to guide us at night!
Be happy everyone!
Have faith!
Praise God!

Psalm

Wonderful things
happen all around us,
celebrating how great God is!
God never hides these fantastic things—
God splashes them on the front page:
love for everyone,
healing from pain and suffering!

Everyone,
get up
and start celebrating—
it's time to party!

Have a great time,
stay up late,
let one another feel the wonderful things
that God has done for us!
Be outrageous!
Dance, leap,
roll over,
get wild and crazy,
and praise God!

God comes to be with us,
to take care of us,
and to make sure that we are happy and alive!

Psalm God is in charge,
and because of that,
some things have to change;
we have to wake up
and realize
that we have a responsibility
to live life with joy,
to be holy,
and to follow God with all our heart.
God,
you love what is good,
and you help us to do good
everywhere we go,
to everyone we meet.

God has always called people
to serve;
God calls us too.
We only have to listen,
pay attention,
and get to work.
Let us now thank God
and remember
that we are called to be holy.
Just like God.

Psalm 100

Be joyful,
be happy,
serve God,
and come close to your Creator!
Recognize God everywhere,
in all things;
remember God made us
who we are.
God leads us,
and we follow.
Get as near to God as you can,
always be thankful,
and bless God in everything you do.
God is good,
so good!
God never stops loving us,
never gives up on us,
forever and ever!

Psalm 101

When I sing,
I will sing for you.
I will sing of all the
great things you do for everyone.
I will try
to be a witness for everyone
in my life:
my family, my friends,
even those who do not like me.
I want to live in a way
that will make you proud
and will help all to see and find
a better way to live for themselves.

I choose to
walk away from bad choices,
to stop gossiping,
and to be more humble,
more like you.

I want to be different
from those who are selfish,
those who lie,
and those who choose sin
over goodness.
Every day
I want to be like you, God,
and I want to help you become
known to everyone.

Psalm  This is a time
when I really need you, God.
Take some time
to be with me—
I need you now.
Everything seems to be falling apart,
everything seems to be going badly.
I feel jinxed;
bad luck seems to follow me everywhere.
I feel bad about the mistakes
I have made;
I wish I could go back
and start over again,
but I am in too deep right now.
And I really need you.

You are in charge,
and sometimes I forget that.
Take charge now,
and help me get my act together.
I know you are watching me
from wherever you are.
If you wanted to,
you could throw me in the trash,
but I know you will not.
Help me to change,
help me to be strong.

Psalm  I want to completely,
totally,
give thanks to you, God!
You always forgive me,
you always heal me,
you save me from death and destruction.
You turn things that are hopeless
into rich possibilities!

You are tender with me,
merciful always,
generous in your love.
You will not keep reminding
me of my sins
nor punish me in the ways
that I deserve to be punished.
Just like a loving mother or father,
you are gentle,
compassionate,
accepting,
incredible.

You are here to save every one of us!
You will come deeply
into our heart,
embrace our shame and guilt
with your two hands,
and set them free,
never to return!
Bless you, God!

Psalm  Everything you make is awesome, God!
The whole world
is full and beautiful because of you!
You make all creation
fabulous:
the clouds, the rain, the wind
all show how great you are!
You created the earth,
a welcome home for us all;
you made the mysterious,
life-giving sea.

If you decide it is time,
you can ask the impossible—
for the sea to climb up the mountains,
down the valleys—
and you can make it stop,
just like that.
You feed everything in need.
With food to eat,
water to drink,
you nourish and help
everything grow.
You decide when the sun rises and sets,
you decide whether or not
we can see the moon,
you help us to wake each day.

I know I sound redundant,
but you are so awesome!
You continually blow me away
and show me new and amazing things!
I want your glory and goodness
to break through everywhere!
I will sing to you,
make music to you forever.
You are a joy for me,
and I bless you.
Alleluia!

Psalm  Remind everyone
about how incredible God is.
Write new songs,
improvise new dances,
make everything new and fresh
to show God's unending miracles!
Look everywhere to see
all the things
God has touched.
Make an accounting,
keep track of all
the amazing works of God!

God is God,
the only judge,
who always keeps promises.
There are so many stories,
so many witnesses:
Joseph and Moses,
Sarah and Rebekah,
Aaron and Abraham,
Miriam and Ruth,
and so many others.
The characters are many,
the situations are different,
but the result is the same:
God holds us close
and refuses to forget us.
God gives us everything we need
if we follow in faith.
Alleluia!

Psalm

God, you are love.
And your love
is beyond any kind of love
that we have received
from anyone else.
Think of me
when you think of your people;
make sure I get to share
in your wonderful plans.

I know that
like others before me,
I sin, and I forget.
But you always forgive.
So remember me, too.
Save me, God, and
gather us all together
to remember you,
to thank you,
and to praise you.
Help us all to sing, "Alleluia!"

Psalm 107

God takes care of all the poor.
There are many stories
that show this.
God is always rescuing
those in need,
no matter where they are.
When people have been in pain,
they have always reached out for God,
and God has come quickly to help them.
They have always been thankful,
as we should be thankful.

No matter what the crisis may be—
hunger, disease, loneliness—
God shows up
and takes care of things.
They have always been thankful,
as we should be thankful.

God can do amazing things:
rivers become sand,
deserts become oceans,
and dry land becomes moist and fertile.
Amazing!
Be happy everyone!
Listen, and pay attention,
and celebrate God's loving ways.

Psalm 108

I will wait no longer—
it is time for me
to sing and rejoice in you, God.
I will sing and share
the news everywhere
about the love that you give.
God,
show the same love
you have shown to me,
and spread it around everywhere!
Make sure everyone
comes to know your strength and power.

Who will help me?
You?
Please don't abandon me now.
Stand by me,
stand by all of us.
We will need no other help.
You are our courage.

Psalm  Liars spread their garbage about me
even though I am good to them.
They don't return love to me.
Even so, I'll still pray for them.

But, God, here's how I really feel.
I hope that they have short, lousy lives,
that they get thrown out on the streets,
that they get ripped off,
that their families disown them.
These people steal from the poor,
cheat the elderly,
and abuse the innocent.
Have no mercy on them, God.
Everything bad that they do
should happen to them.

Help me, God.
I am wounded and hurt.
Show mercy to me,
and bless me.
Stand by me when I am weak and afraid,
stay with me and with all people in need.

Psalm  God says to us,
"Come, sit next to me,
and know
that you will share power with me."
God stands by our side
to destroy all that would harm us.

God is our judge,
God will clear away
all who have victimized us.
We will be the ones
who receive victory,
and we will drink fresh water,
never thirsting again.

Psalm  111

God, you keep your promises.
I thank you from deep down,
with all who are here with me.
It is wonderful to explore
all the incredible things you have done.
Who could possibly forget you?
Who could forget your incredible deeds?
Who could forget you,
a God who nourishes us
and keeps us alive and well?

You are always there for us;
you always have integrity.
You forgive us,
you feed us,
and we are thankful.
We honor you;
it is impossible not to do so.
Praise to you, God!

Psalm 112

If we love God,
if we follow God's way,
we can know true happiness.
This God of ours
is one who only knows mercy,
compassion,
and justice.
When people experience God,
they change,
and they begin to be loving
and fair to people.

When we trust God,
we become strong.
When we support those who are in need,
we become one with God,
and together honor will come our way.
Be warned though:
evil people despise the good,
try to harm them, but,
finally, evil tears itself apart.

Psalm  Praise God!
Praise the name of God!
Forever,
never stop praising God!
From every end of the planet,
come together
and give thanks and praise to God!
God is stronger than any other power;
no one can come close to being God,
only God can be God.

Those who are lost
God will find, and give them a new life;
the poor will be given dignity
and be able to sit in the front row.
Where life was absent,
now it will be teeming with activity!
New life, new energy everywhere!
Alleluia!

Psalm  With you, God,
anything is possible.
You continually turn things
upside down,
and the unthinkable begins to happen:
mountains move,
hills and valleys shake and quiver.
The earth trembles when God speaks,
for God can do unthinkable things:

rocks melt into water
and rivers come forth from the gravel.
With you, God,
anything is possible.

Psalm  G_{od,}
I do not deserve any glory;
you alone deserve praise
because of the way you love,
because of the way you show your truth.
God is God,
and does not have to
answer to anyone.

Some people follow other gods,
gods that are made
of gold and silver,
of status and glitz,
gods that cannot speak truth,
gods that never listen,
gods that are not alive at all.

Our God is an active,
trusting God.
God remembers us,
blesses us,
and shares everything with us.
Everything good we have
belongs to God!
We are alive—
with voices loud and strong,
singing with all we have!
We sing to you, God!
Alleluia!

Psalm  God of love,
I love you.
God fills me to the brim.
God listens whenever I speak.
God pulls my feet from the fire,
lifts me out of despair,
turns my attention to living.
My God is a kind God.
My God is a gentle God.
God takes care of those who are hurting,
and so I am at peace.

When I am downhearted,
sick with fear and worry,
God bends down
and wipes the tears away,
and then takes my hands
and helps me to get up.

How can I ever give back to God?
I raise my cup high
and sing, "Yes, God!"
God, I know you are on our side,
you want us to live.
I am one who wants to serve you;
come and set me free to do so.
I thank you,
I call on you,
and I will keep my promise to you,
everywhere!

Psalm  Sing and praise God!
Nothing less, nothing more—
just thank God with all you have!
God's love is perfect,
faithful,
unending.
Wow!

Psalm

God's love is deep,
deeper than we can imagine!
Let everyone realize—
God's love is deep,
deeper than we can imagine!
Let every person sing out—
God's love is deep,
deeper than we can imagine!
Let everyone who honors God say—
God's love is deep,
deeper than we can imagine!

When I was sad,
God came quickly to help me.
What bad can happen to me
with God by my side?
God helps me,
always.
God is the only one
whom we should trust completely;
everyone else may disappoint us,
whether they intend to or not.
My music is the music of God,
for God gives me the strength to sing.
I shall never die,
I shall always be very much alive,
able to share God's goodness!

People who are
rejected and disliked,
poor and powerless,
and humble enough to call on God—
they are the most favored ones.
God makes this happen,
and we can hardly believe it!
God made this day so wonderful—
let us remember and be glad!
And let us bless those who
help us like God would.

Psalm

Happy are all of us
who make God's law our own.
We won't choose wrongly;
we will follow God.
We cherish God's law
and are thankful for God's guidance.
I take time to reflect
on all that you ask of me;
I know you give guidance
because you love me.
Your path is created for my sake.

God, please be kind,
open my eyes to see clearly
all that you have intended for me.
When you take time to explain them to me,
I am filled with joy,
for you are there for me in everything.
Keep my direction steady,
keep my heart open and gentle,
keep me true to your path.

God, I love your law,
that is what matters to me:
that I always do your will.
Plunge me into the waters of your love,
give me good sense to put faith in you.
Everything I have,
all that I am,
longs to be near you.
I wait for your voice.
I never forget the things you say.
It is what keeps me alive!
Your word is the light
that plows the way forward for me.
I love your law, I follow only you.
My only hope is to praise you.

Psalm  Whenever I am in pain,
God listens,
and speeds toward me,
ready to help.
So, once again,
I need you, God,
to save me from those who hate me.

What do we accomplish
by being so hateful?
So many people deliberately
choose to be cruel.
Why do we have to live like this?
I only want us to be peaceful with one another,
and others want violence.

Psalm  I look to your glorious mountains,
and I wonder, God,
will they be of any help to me?
You are the one who can help me,
and you created everything I see.

I hope that God,
who never sleeps,
will watch over you, always.
The eyes of God never wander;
they are always on us.
Neither the burning sun
nor the evening moon
will be able to hurt us.
God is a protective shield for us,
and our life will be secure.
Every day,
in every way,
God watches out for us.

Psalm

I have overheard others say,
"Let us go and be with God!"
So, God, here we are,
on the boundaries,
waiting to be welcomed by you.
Everyone tries to approach you,
everyone!

Pray for peace
everywhere!
Pray for happiness and safety
everywhere we go.
Greet everyone with peace.
Because God loves everyone,
I hope and pray that only good
will come your way.

Psalm

I often spend hours
looking upward,
looking for you.
Like servants
who listen carefully to their employers,
my eyes stay fixed on you,
waiting for a kind word from you.

Please be merciful,
please be merciful.
I have had enough ridicule,
enough shame thrown my way.

Psalm 124

If God had not been looking out for us,
we would have been destroyed long ago.

Thank God for saving us
time and time again;
for keeping us out of danger
so we could fly away
like a bird escaping the hunter's net.

Our help is God,
God alone,
who created everything around us.

Psalm 125

If we trust God,
we will be strong.
God,
come now and hold us close,
embrace us
always, without fail.
Keep harm
far away from us.
Show your miracles
to those of us who try to do good.
In the midst of all the stench,
bring your peace.

Psalm 126

Dreams do come true!
You have come
and brought clarity
to the craziness of our life.
We are singing,
dancing,
unable to believe what has happened:
you are here with us!
We realize how wonderful this is—
God is truly with us now!

God, help us to remember,
put us back together again.
We have been crying,
but now we are laughing!
God is here!

Psalm 127 If God is not part of the team,
everything we try to do,
everything we try to build,
everything we try to accomplish
will fail.
It is not smart to start early
and to work hard all day
on our own.
If we have God to direct us,
we accomplish twice as much
when we are sleeping.

We are the children of God,
a blessing that only you can provide.
God is happy when we are happy,
and with God
we are able to face anything!

Psalm 128 It is really great to have a God
that we can truly believe in.
Our tables are filled,
loaded with good things,
we are so blessed!
Life sprouts up everywhere
when we give God something to rejoice in.

May God always bless us;
may God give us all a wonderful life.
May we live a long time,
and may we come to know our children,
and their children, too!
Peace!

Psalm  Those who hate us
will try just about anything
to bring us down.
But they never accomplish their goal
because God is on our side.

Let fools stay
fools if they choose to.
Eventually they will lose,
and they will gain nothing.
They will not receive God's blessing.
Praise God!

Psalm  Deep down,
from the bottom of my heart
and the depth of my soul,
I call out to you, God.
Listen,
hear the sound of my voice,
hear the anguish that I share.
God,
if you keep count of all the times
that we fail,
we could never recover.
But you don't do that—
you forgive us over and over.
I am amazed.

I trust you, God.
I really trust you.
More than anyone could ever know,
I trust you.
God, I know you will always be there,
and will always accept me
and forgive me when I fail,
because you are always there
for all who reach out to you.

Psalm  G od,
I try to stay humble.
I try not to brag
and flaunt myself
in front of others.
I try not to reach farther
than I can
and I try to set realistic limits.

I am trying to be calm,
to be peaceful and serene,
just like a child
asleep in its mother's
loving arms.
I hope that all of us can
rest in you.
Always.

Psalm  G od,
come and dwell with us,
and let us see your power.
God chooses us;
God wants to make a home
with all of us,
where we live.

And God will bless us
and take care of us,
for God is the source
of everything we need.
God will give light
on our journey,
feed us when we are hungry.
Full of faith and hope,
may we praise God forever.

Psalm  It is great
when we all get along
and are united with one another!
There is nothing quite like it;
it is like medicine for aches and pains,
soothing deep within our skin,
and it provides healing.
Harmony with one another
is refreshing,
renewing,
and truly a gift—
a gift from God,
a true blessing.

Psalm  When I sleep at night,
God be with me,
to watch over me
and keep me safe.
In my dreams
and when I awake—
I reach out,
blessing you, God.
God,
who creates everything,
bless us always.

Psalm  God, no one is like you,
no one compares to you!
You are totally good,
completely loving.
There are others
who try to capture my attention,
but they do not come
close to what you are
and who you are.
Whatever you want from me,
I will gladly give it.

Just as you freed the Israelites
from captivity in Egypt,
you seek to release people
when they are victimized,
you bring a smile
to those who are sad,
you heal those
who need your care.

People who ignore you,
who worship their possessions,
prestige, or power,
are living in a fool's paradise.
All who follow you
and pay attention to your path—
they are truly blessed.
Alleluia!

Psalm  God is so good!
God's love is for real!
God is the one who gives us life!
God's love is for real!
God designs everything!
God's love is for real!
God shines through everything!
God's love is for real!
The sun rises, the moon lights up the night!
God's love is for real!
God leads us through difficult times!
God's love is for real!
God tramples those who hurt us!
God's love is for real!
God remembers us when we are alone!
God's love is for real!
God keeps us safe through everything!
God's love is for real!
God frees us from our inner prisons!
God's love is for real!
God accepts us as we are!
God's love is for real!

God feeds the hungry!
God's love is for real!
God is great! Thank God!
God's love is for real!

Psalm  Broken, alone, scared, and hopeless,
we despair that things will ever get better.
We never laugh anymore.
Fun is unheard of.
We are jokes,
objects of rejection,
subjects of abuse.
We feel like strangers,
ignored by you, God.

Help us to plow through it all
and to see your presence with us
in this.
Right now
I feel alone and grow cynical.
What is there to feel good about?
Even so, if I forget you,
may my hands shrivel up
and my tongue stay stuck in my mouth.
As for our enemies,
in my heart I imagine an unspeakable fate.
God, do with them what you will.

Psalm  I thank you, God,
for you really do hear me.
You listen to me,
and I will keep singing to you,
I will keep praying to you,
and I will try always
to remember this
and be thankful.

You are with us everywhere,
all the time.

Though it seems sometimes
that you are far away,
you keep an eye on everything,
not like a divine prison warden
but like a loving parent.
When I am in danger,
you keep me alive,
you reach out for me,
you hold me tight.
God,
I need you to speak on my behalf.
If you truly love me,
keep me close to you—
don't leave me,
for you made me who I am.

Psalm  God,
you know me better
than I know myself.
Wherever I go
you are right there.
If I walk one way,
you walk with me;
and wherever I have been,
you know it well.
While I am trying to figure out
what I am going to say,
you already know what it is.
You place your hand on me,
and I feel loved.
It is too much to take in!

Is there no way to hide from you?
Is there any place where I can escape?
I go high—you are there.
I go down low—you are there.

If I could fly, you would be nearby;
If I were to swim miles and miles,
you would take hold of me
and set me in the right direction.

You have made every part of me;
you were there creating me
in my mother's womb
before I was born.
All this is much more than I can fathom!
You watched every step of how I was formed;
you saw my body grow,
all according to your plan.
You knew the direction of my life,
even before my life began.
Your mind is so deep—
beyond my understanding!

Find me,
study me,
and look deeply into my thoughts.
Lead me, God.
Lead me.

Psalm  God,
I need you.
Again.
There are people out there
who want to hurt me.
They spew poisoned words,
spreading lies about me.
Sometimes I want to hurt myself,
because even I don't like myself
that much.

I sometimes feel
that I will never amount to much;
I sometimes think my foes
are right about me.
Please help me to think differently,
help me to forget their version of me.
I know you are on my side,
especially when I feel weak.

Psalm  **141**

Hurry, God!
Quickly,
do not delay—
I need you now!
My prayer right now is like smoke rising.
My hands reach high for you.
God, look out for me,
watch what comes out of my mouth.
I don't ever want to say anything
that would hurt someone else.
I don't ever want to participate
in anything
that is intended to cause harm.

If my good friends correct me,
I accept it with thanks.
But I do not want to accept
any gift from someone
who would harm me or someone else.
I pray that I never become like them.
God,
I need you—
don't run from me,
don't trick me.
Let me escape the test.

Psalm **142**

I feel all alone right now,
deserted by my friends,
feeling as if I really don't
matter at all.
I pray, God,
that you will listen,
for I have nowhere else to go.
I am feeling overwhelmed
by everything right now.

Help me, please.
Free me from thinking
that I am trapped,
that there is no way out.

Then I can be happy again.
Thank you for listening.
Thank you for being so kind.

Psalm  God, hear me,
I mean, really hear me.
I know I don't deserve it,
but please do not judge me too hard.

I feel trapped,
I don't have the strength to go on,
I feel spent and unable even to move.
I need you to speak to me now.
I will offer you all my energy
if you will just point me
in the right direction.

The evil voices are not
the voices of other people;
they are the voices in my head,
and I need you to clear my mind
and set me free from the clatter.
I belong to you.
Bring me back.

Psalm  Sometimes
I don't understand
why you care for us.
You constantly reach down
and choose to be with us—
I find that absolutely amazing!

I plan to show you how happy I am;
I will sing and share
with everyone I can
because you are always there,
ready to take care of me.
When I am hungry,
you feed me.

When I cannot breathe,
you give me space and clean air.
With you there is no isolation,
for you bless us with great things!

Psalm  **H**oly One,
Mentor and Teacher!
No name can express
how great you are.
Throughout all time
each generation tells
of what you have done.
When I take time to think about it,
I am filled with happiness.
You, God, are always helpful,
always generous,
always listening,
ready to be there for us
no matter what.

We are grateful
that we have such a God;
we feel so blessed
and filled with power
unknown before!
You, God, will always support us
and help us to keep moving
when we feel paralyzed.
Those who look to you, God,
receive your unconditional love.
Your hands are never closed to us—
always open, ready to embrace us.
You always keep your word,
you are always nearby,
you help us to feel alive and worthy!
I will praise you, always!

Psalm  By now I should know
that I cannot depend totally
on other people—
they are human,
they are frail,
and they are apt to make mistakes.
But I should always look to you,
depend on you, God,
and remember that
you alone provide all that we need.
When we are weak,
you are strong.
When we are blind to the pain in others,
you open our eyes to see them more clearly.
You comfort those in deep pain
and protect those who are in danger.
Thank you, God!
We should praise you all the time
and pass the word on to everyone!
Alleluia!

Psalm  God, you are the one,
you are the reason
we are so fortunate,
so blessed,
and on the right road!
You keep picking us up
when we fall;
you keep binding our wounds
and teaching us to heal others.
Everyone,
we should always thank God!
God continues to help us grow,
and rains down love
to keep us going.

God is strong,
and we need that strength
every day of our life.
When we feel the cold of winter,
and the cold of bitterness,
God warms us.
You, God, melt the ice in our heart,
and the heat of your love remains.
Keep speaking,
keep prodding us,
keep sharing your wisdom with us.
Alleluia!

Psalm  Everything that is alive,
everyone who can breathe,
stand up,
speak out,
and let everyone know how much
you praise God!
God who calls us forth
from nothing,
God who continually moves in us
is worthy of our thanks and praise!

Fire and rain—praise God!
Mountains, hills,
rivers, streams—
come now and praise God!
Leaders and elders—praise God!
Young men and women—praise God!
God strengthens us,
God loves us,
God is for us—praise God!
Alleluia!

Psalm 149

Everyone come together now,
and join with one voice
to sing to God—
not the same old song
but a new song!
A song with new vitality,
a song with new energy,
loud and strong!
God loves to help us;
celebrate with God,
right now!
Sing until you can't
sing anymore!
God gives us the power
to share in the glory!
Alleluia!

Psalm 150

It is time to sing Alleluia!
Sing and dance it
in every way possible!
Bring the whole band together—
praise God with horns,
with guitars and drums!
Praise God with the latest dance!
Praise God with our voices!

Praise God with good choices
and with unconditional love for one another!

Praise God with everything we have—
with our entire life—
living well,
the best we can!
With full voice, sing out!
Alleluia!
Alleluia!

Prayer and Special Need Index

When I am angry
Psalms 10, 13, 22, 58, 69, 73, 77

When I am being called to be just
Psalms 11, 14, 15, 18, 20, 25, 40, 45, 53, 68, 69, 72, 85, 97, 99, 101, 112, 113, 119

When I am dealing with desires
Psalms 5, 17, 23, 40, 49, 57, 95, 124, 138

When I am discovering something new
Psalms 12, 36, 84, 104, 126, 139

When I am enjoying life
Psalms 9, 29, 33, 34, 47, 66, 84, 108, 148, 150

When I am experiencing the family of God
Psalms 15, 33, 68, 100, 101, 108, 122, 126, 128, 133

When I am fearful
Psalms 3, 4, 6, 7, 10, 13, 21, 22, 23, 27, 28, 34, 38, 54, 55, 56, 57, 59, 64, 70, 77, 90, 91, 102, 121, 142

When I am feeling fulfilled and content
Psalms 8, 15, 17, 29, 30, 34, 68, 84, 91, 93, 100, 116, 126, 127

When I am feeling lonely
Psalms 13, 22, 56, 69, 77, 88, 91, 102, 121

When I am feeling peaceful
Psalms 4, 16, 29, 62, 85, 112, 122, 131, 134

When I am feeling thankful
Psalms 1, 8, 9, 16, 18, 27, 33, 34, 45, 72, 78, 89, 96, 103, 108, 115, 133, 145, 147

When I am going through a time of growth
Psalms 1, 20, 25, 31, 41, 57, 121

When I am going through new beginnings
Psalms 8, 16, 24, 26, 40, 56, 97, 104, 108, 117, 118, 126, 147

When I am grieving
Psalms 6, 8, 13, 23, 31, 38, 41, 61, 77, 88, 91, 102, 121

When I am happy
Psalms 8, 9, 16, 18, 23, 33, 34, 68, 84, 96, 103, 108, 126

When I am in need
Psalms 3, 4, 5, 6, 7, 10, 13, 16, 17, 24, 26, 28, 30, 31, 32, 35, 39, 42–43, 51, 55, 56, 57, 61, 64, 69, 70, 83, 85, 88, 90, 91, 102, 109, 123, 124, 142

When I am in need of comfort
Psalms 23, 27, 31, 36, 41, 56, 59, 70, 86, 89, 90, 91, 111, 121, 124, 139, 142

When I am in need of recovery
Psalms 22, 23, 27, 31, 32, 33, 40, 41, 42–43, 51, 54, 55, 56, 57, 62, 70, 71, 91, 103, 111, 121, 130, 140

When I am in need of renewal
Psalms 51, 53, 70, 95, 96, 101, 104, 116, 119, 122, 126, 147

When I am in pain
Psalms 7, 10, 12, 13, 31, 32, 34, 39, 57, 69, 77, 102, 109, 121, 123

When I am in trouble
Psalms 3, 5, 6, 7, 12, 13, 22, 23, 31, 32, 39, 41, 55, 57, 62, 64, 70, 77, 83, 91, 123, 132, 142, 143

When I am seeking God's will in my life
Psalms 15, 16, 19, 20, 23, 24, 25, 26, 36, 40, 69, 80, 95, 100, 101, 103, 112, 132, 137

When I am stressful
Psalms 3, 6, 7, 22, 23, 26, 28, 31, 32, 39, 42–43, 56, 59, 61, 64, 83, 88, 91, 102, 121, 131, 142

When I am struggling with my own integrity
Psalms 12, 15, 19, 26, 50, 57, 68, 85, 101, 103, 109

When I am trying to get through a difficult time
Psalms 4, 5, 6, 13, 16, 21, 22, 23, 30, 31, 32, 41, 42–43, 54, 56, 61, 64, 69, 77, 119, 121, 123, 124, 132, 137

When I am waiting
Psalms 4, 5, 13, 17, 22, 27, 33, 42–43, 63

When I experience God's promise for me
Psalms 1, 3, 4, 8, 9, 11, 12, 15, 16, 17, 19, 20, 25, 27, 30, 32, 36, 46, 55, 57, 71, 75, 81, 82, 84, 89, 93, 99, 100, 103, 105, 106, 108, 111, 114, 119, 124, 126, 130, 133, 147

When I experience God's Reign in my life
Psalms 8, 9, 24, 27, 33, 48, 67, 71, 81, 82, 93, 100, 101, 104, 105, 106, 107, 108, 113, 124, 136, 147, 149

When I experience the power of God
Psalms 1, 2, 4, 8, 9, 11, 12, 19, 29, 31, 33, 34, 47, 67, 71, 75, 81, 82, 93, 99, 103, 104, 105, 106, 107, 108, 109, 111, 113, 114, 118, 126, 136, 145, 147, 149, 150

When I feel confident in God
Psalms 1, 2, 4, 8, 9, 11, 12, 16, 18, 19, 23, 25, 27, 31, 36, 46, 47, 48, 54, 55, 75, 81, 82, 86, 89, 93, 104, 105, 107, 111, 114, 121, 124, 127, 130, 135, 139, 144, 147, 149

When I feel ecstatically happy
Psalms 8, 9, 18, 29, 33, 66, 96, 98, 104, 108, 118, 126, 135, 136, 145, 148, 149, 150

When I feel free
Psalms 8, 9, 11, 12, 18, 29, 30, 34, 68, 108, 112, 116, 128

When I feel generous and giving
Psalms 29, 36, 40, 116

When I feel God's friendship
Psalms 9, 11, 25, 27, 31, 34, 68, 69, 71, 81, 100, 108, 112, 116, 124, 127, 128, 133, 134, 147, 149

When I feel God's protection
Psalms 2, 7, 11, 12, 16, 19, 20, 23, 26, 27, 29, 31, 33, 36, 46, 54, 62, 71, 81, 82, 91, 93, 103, 105, 106, 107, 111, 114, 121, 124, 127, 130, 132, 134, 147

When I feel or am alone
Psalms 10, 13, 22, 31, 56, 61, 69, 83, 139, 142

When I feel or seek God's tenderness
Psalms 1, 3, 9, 16, 23, 36, 57, 86, 91, 103, 127, 132, 140

When I feel powerless
Psalms 3, 12, 13, 16, 31, 32, 40, 42–43, 51, 57, 64, 70, 77, 102, 107, 109, 121, 123, 139, 140, 142, 143

When I feel the call to serve
Psalms 2, 15, 20, 40, 68, 97

When I feel the Spirit in my life
Psalms 93, 104

When I feel the wonder of God
Psalms 8, 9, 11, 18, 27, 34, 36, 47, 48, 66, 67, 71, 81, 92, 93, 96, 99, 100, 103, 105, 107, 113, 114, 124, 125, 126, 135, 136, 145, 147, 148, 149, 150

When I find it hard to accept God's love
  Psalms 4, 16, 23, 25, 31, 69, 84,
102, 112, 119

When I find it hard to love myself
  Psalm 100

When I find it hard to receive
  Psalms 4, 12, 29, 84, 100

When I focus on my gifts and the gifts
of others
  Psalms 19, 20, 34, 36, 40, 72, 84,
103, 111

When I have to face my dark side
  Psalms 6, 7, 13, 14, 22, 38, 39, 51,
53, 88, 91, 123, 137

When I have to face responsibility
  Psalms 15, 20, 32, 40, 67, 68, 97,
100, 101, 112, 113, 117, 119, 137

When I need acceptance
  Psalms 16, 27, 36, 40, 84, 100, 131,
139

When I need and want to follow God
  Psalms 15, 16, 19, 20, 23, 24, 25,
26, 27, 30, 31, 36, 40, 42–43, 51, 81,
101, 104, 108, 112, 116, 117, 122,
124, 127, 137, 138, 139, 144

When I need assurance
  Psalms 1, 2, 3, 4, 7, 12, 14, 17, 18,
21, 23, 26, 34, 37, 44, 46, 54, 59, 102,
106, 111, 124, 126, 127, 144, 149

When I need courage
  Psalms 2, 3, 5, 11, 13, 14, 15, 17, 22,
31, 40, 57, 75, 109, 121, 124, 132, 137

When I need direction
  Psalms 5, 12, 13, 15, 16, 17, 19, 20,
23, 24, 27, 31, 36, 40, 41, 51, 57, 63,
71, 95, 97, 104, 112, 116, 119, 121,
122, 123

When I need discipline
  Psalms 4, 15, 19, 20, 26, 40, 50, 51,
95, 97, 112, 117, 119, 123, 137

When I need faith
  Psalms 4, 6, 8, 10, 12, 13, 16, 17,
21, 23, 24, 27, 31, 34, 55, 61, 65, 77,
91, 95, 105, 106, 107, 109, 121, 132,
139, 144, 145

When I need forgiveness or when it is
hard to forgive
  Psalms 23, 30, 41, 51, 123, 130, 143

When I need guidance
  Psalms 16, 17, 19, 20, 24, 31, 36,
40, 56, 57, 95, 102, 112, 119, 134,
138, 139

When I need healing
  Psalms 4, 6, 21, 23, 30, 32, 34, 36,
41, 51, 61, 77, 91, 103, 113, 121, 123,
126, 143

When I need hope
  Psalms 1, 13, 16, 20, 21, 26, 46, 56,
64, 77, 107, 124

When I need patience
  Psalms 13, 33, 127

When I need strength
  Psalms 3, 6, 8, 12, 20, 23, 26, 31,
39, 40, 46, 51, 54, 57, 70, 71, 91, 102,
107, 109, 111, 119, 120, 121, 124,
125, 140, 142, 143

When I need to be calm
  Psalms 16, 23, 27, 36, 40, 56, 57,
89, 90, 131, 139

When I need to be challenged
  Psalms 13, 17, 20, 40, 72, 95, 97,
122

When I need to be honest
  Psalms 13, 17, 22, 26, 49, 50

When I need to be more open to God
  Psalms 4, 16, 19, 23, 24, 31, 63, 81,
95, 116, 119, 124, 134

When I need to be more tolerant
  Psalm 13

When I need to empower others
Psalms 4, 40, 81, 95, 97, 101, 104, 122

When I need to feel safe
Psalms 3, 7, 11, 12, 16, 20, 23, 26, 27, 30, 31, 37, 41, 54, 56, 57, 62, 70, 76, 84, 91, 103, 107, 121, 140

When I need to let go in love
Psalms 18, 34

When I need to let go in prayer
Psalms 5, 51, 134

When I need to let go of my anger
Psalms 6, 13, 22, 38, 39, 51

When I need to let go of my fear
Psalms 3, 12, 16, 23, 26, 32, 38, 41, 46, 54, 55, 57, 62, 64, 90, 121, 127, 134

When I need to let go of my guilt and shame
Psalms 23, 31, 32, 38, 41, 71, 103, 123

When I need to let go of perfection in myself and others
Psalms 30, 40, 51, 139

When I need to listen to God
Psalms 5, 16, 42–43, 63, 95, 131, 143, 144

When I need to make a decision
Psalms 26, 27, 40, 117, 119, 122

When I need to recommit to God
Psalms 15, 17, 19, 20, 24, 26, 27, 40, 44, 95, 97, 101, 112, 119, 122, 137, 138, 143, 145

When I need to seek or speak the truth
Psalms 20, 24, 26, 34, 36, 50, 101, 121, 136

When I need to surrender and let go
Psalms 16, 26, 32, 37, 40, 57, 63, 88, 95, 103, 112, 124, 139

When I need to think clearly
Psalms 4, 11, 32, 40, 95, 97, 131

When I need to trust God
Psalms 1, 3, 4, 7, 8, 12, 13, 17, 23, 24, 25, 27, 31, 32, 36, 37, 49, 52, 54, 55, 65, 71, 76, 91, 103, 107, 111, 119, 121, 124, 125, 130, 144

When I or others are suffering from sickness
Psalms 22, 23, 27, 41, 55, 91, 121, 146

When I think or worry about the future
Psalms 12, 16, 18, 21, 24, 26, 28, 40, 56, 61, 64, 71, 90, 116, 139

When it is evening
Psalms 27, 121, 141

When it is late at night
Psalms 4, 16, 88, 91, 131, 134

When it is morning
Psalms 5, 8, 24, 36, 62, 63, 95, 100, 105, 143

When I want and need God's blessing
Psalms 1, 4, 8, 12, 17, 18, 20, 26, 36, 72, 86, 103, 104, 111, 112, 115, 126, 127, 133, 134

When I want to be close to God
Psalms 16, 23, 27, 31, 84, 116, 124, 126, 128, 131, 134

When I want to celebrate God's word
Psalms 13, 19, 95, 130, 147

When I want to celebrate the Resurrection
Psalms 47, 66, 98, 104, 105, 118, 126, 136, 147, 149, 150

When I want to give glory to God
Psalms 8, 9, 24, 29, 33, 34, 47, 48, 66, 67, 81, 96, 98, 104, 105, 108, 118, 126, 135, 136, 147, 148, 150

When I want to know God in a deeper way
Psalms 4, 12, 16, 19, 24, 25, 27, 30, 33, 36, 62, 130, 139

When I want to meditate
Psalms 8, 23, 42–43, 131, 139

When I want to minister
Psalms 15, 20, 40, 68, 72, 97, 101, 113, 116, 117

When I want to move forward in my life
Psalms 16, 19, 20, 40, 51, 95, 97, 104, 118, 119, 122, 126, 138, 144, 148, 149

When I want to praise God
Psalms 8, 9, 18, 29, 33, 34, 47, 48, 66, 67, 71, 81, 86, 96, 97, 99, 105, 108, 113, 118, 124, 126, 135, 136, 144, 145, 147, 148, 149, 150

When I want to pray for others
Psalms 100, 103, 104, 112, 117, 121, 122, 148, 150

When I want to witness to others
Psalms 15, 26, 34, 97, 101, 103, 113, 117, 147, 149

When someone dies
Psalms 22, 23, 91, 131

When there is conflict
Psalms 3, 6, 13, 22, 32, 39, 59, 109

Liturgical Index

Advent
Psalms 24, 25, 72, 80, 85, 89, 122, 126, 146

Christmas
Psalms 80, 89, 96, 97, 128

Epiphany
Psalm 72

Baptism of the Lord
Psalm 29

Ash Wednesday
Psalm 51

Lent
Psalms 19, 23, 25, 27, 32, 33, 51, 91, 95, 103, 116, 126, 130, 137

Easter Vigil
Psalms 16, 19, 30, 33, 42–43, 51, 104, 118

Easter Sunday
Psalms 66, 118, 136

Easter Season
Psalms 4, 16, 23, 27, 30, 33, 66, 67, 97, 98, 100, 118, 136, 145, 150

Ascension
Psalm 47

Pentecost
Psalm 104

Trinity Sunday
Psalms 8, 33

The Body and Blood of Christ (Corpus Christi)
Psalm 116

Christ the King
Psalms 23, 122

All Saints
Psalm 24

Ritual and Sacrament Index

Anointing of the Sick
  Psalms 6, 25, 27, 34, 42–43, 63, 71, 86, 103, 123

Celebrations of Ministry
  Psalms 23, 84, 89, 96, 100, 116, 117

Christian Initiation and Confirmation
  Psalms 34, 66, 104, 117, 118, 136

Funeral
  Psalms 23, 25, 27, 42–43, 51, 63, 103, 116, 121, 122, 123, 126, 130

Marriage
  Psalms 8, 16, 33, 34, 103, 112, 128, 145, 148

Reconciliation
  Psalms 8, 13, 25, 31, 32, 36, 51, 95, 123, 139